STORIES FROM
THE HINDU WORLD

written by

Jamila Gavin

illustrated by

Joanna Troughton

Macdonald

Managing Editor : Belinda Hollyer
Book Editors : Barbara Tombs, Jenny Vaughan
Designer : Liz Black
Production Controller : Rosemary Bishop

Consultant : S.L. Naib, Headmaster, Victoria County
Junior School, Wellingborough

A MACDONALD BOOK

© text Jamila Gavin 1986
© illustrations Macdonald & Co (Publishers) Ltd 1986

First published in Great Britain in 1986 by
Macdonald & Co (Publishers) Ltd
London & Sydney
A BPCC plc company

Printed in Great Britain by
Purnell Book Production Ltd
Member of the BPCC Group

Macdonald & Co (Publishers) Ltd
Greater London House
Hampstead Road
London NW1 7QX

British Library Cataloguing in Publication Data
Gavin, Jamila
 Stories from the Hindu world.
 1. Mythology, Hindu —— Juvenile literature
 I. Title
 294.5'13   BL1145.5

 ISBN 0-356-11509-7

CONTENTS

How the World Began

This is one of the oldest Hindu creation stories. In this story, Lord Brahma is the Creator. While he sleeps, nothing exists, but when he wakes he creates the universe. This happens over and over again, in a never-ending cycle.

Before the world began, there was only a Lotus flower floating on a Sea of Milk. Within its creamy, magical petals God himself, Lord Brahma, lay sleeping peacefully.

He had been sleeping for more than eternity. While he was asleep the Universe couldn't exist; but as his eyelids opened, there was a trembling over the endless milky surface of the Sea. Lord Brahma awoke, and Life began once more.

Lord Brahma looked around and saw how lonely he was. He was so lonely that he wept. Great tears rolled down his cheeks. Some fell into the sea and

became the Earth. Others he brushed away and they became the Air and Sky. Then he stretched. He stretched upwards and his body became the Universe, and outwards to create Day and Night. He stretched and created Twilight and Moonlight; Fire, Wind and Rain. He created the dry seasons and the wet seasons, and then he created the gods.

The gods of Darkness were called Asuras. Their friends were demons, goblins, giants and serpents.

The gods of Light were called Devas. They shone with beauty and goodness, and their friends were fairies, nymphs, angels and saints.

In the Sea of Milk was a miraculous element called amrit. Anyone who drank it stayed young forever. The Devas wanted to get the amrit out of the ocean and keep it for themselves. The Asuras too wanted to get the amrit out of the ocean and keep it for themselves. But the only way to get it was by churning the Sea of Milk, and neither the Devas nor the Asuras could manage that alone. Enemies as they were, they had to work together.

To churn the ocean, they needed a churning rod and rope. But what rod and rope could they find, powerful enough to churn the Sea of Milk?

They came to a great mountain which rose out of the sea. It was the Mountain Mandrachal. 'This is the churning rod!' cried the Devas.

The Asuras came with a monstrous serpent, long and winding, with a hooded head and darting tongue. 'This is our rope,' they said. They wound the serpent round the mountain. Then the Asuras took hold of the serpent's terrible head, and the Devas

grasped his long, thrashing tail. Between them they began to tug to and fro, to and fro. The mountain began to churn the sea. The Ocean of Milk began to froth and foam. Steam poured from the serpent's mouth. Lightning flashed. Fire and rain swirled about. Still they heaved this way and that, until at last the Sea of Milk was one great whirlpool. It began to turn to butter, and at last, there was the precious amrit glistening in the thickening waves.

Suddenly an angel came flying over the ocean carrying a golden goblet. He swooped down, and filled it with amrit.

The Devas and Asuras rushed towards the angel ready to fight for the amrit. But the great God did not want the Asuras to have the amrit, lest the demons should have too much power.

Then one of the demons disguised himself as a Deva. Standing between the Sun and Moon, he reached out. The angel gave him the golden goblet. Immediately he tipped back his head and drank.

The Sun and Moon saw this. 'Stop!' they cried. 'That is the terrible demon, Rahu!' The magic liquid was just trickling down Rahu's throat, when the God of All struck off his head. The body plunged downwards, dead, but because the amrit had reached his throat, the head could live for ever. It soared up into the sky, roaring and howling.

The Devas and the Asuras flew at each other in fury. A fearful battle began. Burning rocks and mountains, thunderbolts and fiery arrows flew through the sky. But the Devas were more powerful. Gradually the Asuras and demons were defeated. Thousands lay dead and dying, while others crawled away to hide in the bowels of the earth, and the caverns of the sea.

Of all the demons, only Rahu's head would live for ever. His gaping mouth chased the Sun and the Moon around the heavens. If he caught one and swallowed it, there was an eclipse, but only until it slipped through his throat and out into the sky again.

How Lord Shiva Became Blue-throated

Lord Shiva is the Destroyer of Evil. If you look at Indian paintings where he is shown, you will see that he always has a blue throat. This story explains why.

Demons beware when Lord Shiva dances! He whirls his trident and lightning flashes. Never look at the third eye burning in the middle of his forehead, for it shrivels all within its gaze. When a terrible tiger tried to tear him to pieces, he just smiled and stripped it of its skin with the nail of his little finger. When a fearful snake tried to poison him, he hung it round his neck as a garland, and when a demon dwarf came with a club, Shiva jumped on his back and danced. When Lord Shiva dances, demons beware, for his rhythm is a trap and his dance is the dance of the cosmos.

In the beginning when the ocean was being churned, the gods and demons were watching. Shiva too was watching. He saw how Vasuki the serpent was used as a rope, wound round the mountain Mandrachal. The gods and demons twisted the mountain like a churning stick, so violently that fire and steam swirled around it. The whole mountain would have been destroyed had not Lord Indra sent rain-filled clouds of cooling water.

This was the churning of creation. Wonderful things rose out of the waves. There came the marvellous cow; the goddess of wine; the tree of

paradise whose scent filled the world; there came nymphs called apsaras who went to live in Indra's heaven, and there came the moon. Still the churning went on. Now there appeared a white horse which the Preserver Lord Vishnu took for his steed, and an elephant for Lord Indra to ride on.

Suddenly, the most wonderful creation of all rose out of the churning – the goddess, Lakshmi. She rose upwards, with her four golden arms stretched out to bring good fortune, love and prosperity.

'She must be ours!' cried the demons.

'She is my queen,' said Lord Vishnu.

The gods and the demons twisted the mountain even more violently, and Vasuki the serpent suffered terrible torment. He opened his jaws, and torrents of blue venom poured out. The whole world would have been destroyed, but Shiva leapt forward and gulped down the poison. The deadly liquid burned in his throat, and when Shiva threw his head back, everyone saw that his throat was blue. But the world had been saved. The goddess Lakshmi sat joyfully on Lord Vishnu's knee, and Lord Shiva became known from then on as 'Nilkanth' – the blue-throated one.

Indra, the Dragon-slayer

Indra is the thunder god and bringer of rain. There are several versions of this story, which tells how he fights the dragon and demons. Once he has won the fight, he can release the rain clouds, which bring life to the countryside.

Vritra the dragon lay within the dark caverns of the earth, while the demons prepared for battle with the gods. They were confident, for with Vritra on their side no one could beat them.

The gods cried out to Lord Brahma, Creator of all Living Things: 'If Vritra is not killed, the demons will take over the universe!'

Lord Brahma replied, 'There is a rishi whose name is Dadhicha. If he will sacrifice his life, you can make a weapon from his bones to destroy the dragon.'

The noble rishi Dadhicha lay down and gave up his life. The gods took his bones and made a mighty thunderstone. But who among them was brave enough to use this weapon?

'I will!' cried Indra, the God of Thunder, fighter of the Drought Demons, son of Mother Earth and Father Heaven. He was a wild, reckless, boisterous young god, who loved to drink soma, the nectar of the gods, and to ride over the sky with his friends the Wind Spirits. With flashing eyes and bellowing laugh he took up the thunderstone. 'I will slay the dragon!'

He snatched the bowl of soma and gulped it down. Immediately he felt a wondrous strength.

'Come!' he shouted to his friends.

The Wind Spirits, in gold armour, leaped into their deer-drawn chariots. Indra sat astride his elephant. They charged across the heavens, with Indra whirling the thunderstone about his head. The demons came towards them, with horrible screams.

Then Vritra rose out of the earth like a volcano. His pointed scales were terrible as mountain peaks and fire spurted out in all directions. Battle began. Soon thousands of gods lay dead or scattered. Only Indra could save them. As he drew nearer, his face began to scorch and his hair to smoulder. Clenching the thunderstone, he gazed in horror. Where should he strike? Desperately he swung the weapon and then hurled it. It arched through the sky and disappeared into the writhing coils of the dragon.

Indra fled. He was sure he had failed, for the monster was shrieking behind him. Filled with shame, he flung himself into a cave beneath a lake.

But he had dealt the death blow. The gods shouted joyfully as Vritra shuddered and died. At once rain poured from the sky, and Indra came out of his hiding place, singing at the top of his voice.

Manu's Ark

There are flood stories in many parts of the world. The Bible story of Noah is probably the best known. The Hindu story of Manu, the first man to live on earth, tells the story of a flood at the very beginning of creation.

Manu, the first man on earth, stood praying in a stream. For years, he had stood on one leg with his arms upstretched to heaven. Nothing, it seemed, could disturb him.

Then one day a little fish nudged his ankle. 'Manu! Help! A big fish is trying to eat me!' Even though Manu's mind was on the Meaning of Life, the Universe and the Cause of Everything, he took pity on the little creature. He scooped it up in a pitcher.

The fish began to grow. It grew and grew so he put it in a tank. It grew and grew, so he heaved it along to the sacred River Ganga. But soon it was squashed between the banks of the holy river. 'Take me to the sea,' gasped the fish, 'or else I'll die!'

Praying to Lord Brahma for strength, Manu hauled it to the ocean. With a wriggle of joy it plunged into the billowing waves.

'Thank you, Manu!' it cried. 'You have saved my life! Listen! Lord Brahma, the Creator, is not pleased with this evil world. He wants to destroy everything and start again. Do as I say, and you will be saved.'

Manu listened. Then he went out and built a massive boat. He went to every part of the world and collected the seed of every living thing, including the

seed of seven holy rishis, the gods and the demons. He carried them all back to the ark, and waited.

The destruction began. Seven blazing suns appeared in the sky, burning fiercely. Wind and fire came like greedy tongues, licking round the world, gobbling everything in their path. Great, black clouds rolled across the sky. With a mighty crack, they split open, and down came the rain.

It rained for twelve years and Lord Brahma destroyed everything except Manu and his ark.

When at last the rain stopped, how lonely Manu felt! The water stretched from one horizon to another. Suddenly he saw a horned fish swimming towards him. Overjoyed, Manu swung a rope over its horns.

Year after year the fish dragged the ark across the never-ending water, until one day, rising out of the misty waves, Manu saw the tip of a mountain. The ark bumped to a standstill on the rocky slopes.

Then the fish spoke. 'I am Brahma, Lord of all Living Things. I saved you from the flood, Manu, so that, when the waters drop, you can create life again.

So Manu set about creating all living things from the seeds on the ark. Soon all the rivers, seas, jungles and deserts were filled with life. The gods were back in their heavens, the demons returned to the underworld. The seven rishis began to pray, and Manu stood on the earth again and thanked God.

How Lord Agni Tried to Hide

This story tells how Lord Agni, the God of Fire, creator of the sun as well as the humble fire in the hearth was afraid. Anyone could put out his fire . . . so he made sure that the gods realized how important he was.

The gods hunted everywhere. Where was Lord Agni, the God of Fire, whose light brightens even the darkest corners of the universe, and whose power terrified the demons? No one could find him.

Nobody guessed that he was hiding in the waters under the earth. Then a little frog complained. 'If it's Agni you're looking for, he's in the water. I can't swim without being scalded!'

Agni cursed the frog for giving him away. 'From now on, you will have no tongue and no taste!'

The gods came to the waters to find Agni had fled. They comforted the weeping frog. 'Never mind,' they said. 'You will make different noises and the earth will always look after you.'

Agni hid in a fig tree, but an elephant caught a glimpse of the blazing light shrivelling its leaves. 'Come quickly!' he cried to the gods. 'Agni is here!'

The gods rushed over, but Agni had gone. 'Agni

says that from now on my tongue will only bend backwards,' wept the poor elephant.

'Never mind,' comforted the gods. 'The sound you make will be as glorious as trumpets!'

Agni looked desperately for somewhere to hide, and swooped inside a hollow sami tree. But a parrot had seen him, and flew to the gods.

'Agni's hiding inside the sami tree!' it cried.

The gods saw flames shoot out of the top of the tree as Agni cursed the parrot. 'From now on,' he roared, 'you will never speak!'

'Don't worry,' said the gods. 'Your sound will be beautiful. It is "ka!" – the sound young children make.'

'Ka!' cried the parrot gratefully, and flew away.

The gods called out: 'Why do you hide from us? We have looked and longed for you in heaven and earth. We need your fiery weapons to fight the demons, and without your sacred flame, who can make sacrifices to enter into heaven? Agni! We need you!'

Agni was agitated. 'That's all very well!' he retorted. 'But what is my reward? You make use of me, then blow me out. I had three brothers who served you but when you were done with them, you extinguished them. Will you do the same to me?'

'From now on,' said the gods, 'this sami tree is your dwelling place. Anyone who rubs two of its sticks together shall give birth to you. You will live as long as there is a spark of life in the universe.'

Agni was satisfied. From then on he became the messenger between heaven and earth. No hearth was too humble for his flickering flame, and with his bright light, no one need ever again fear the dark.

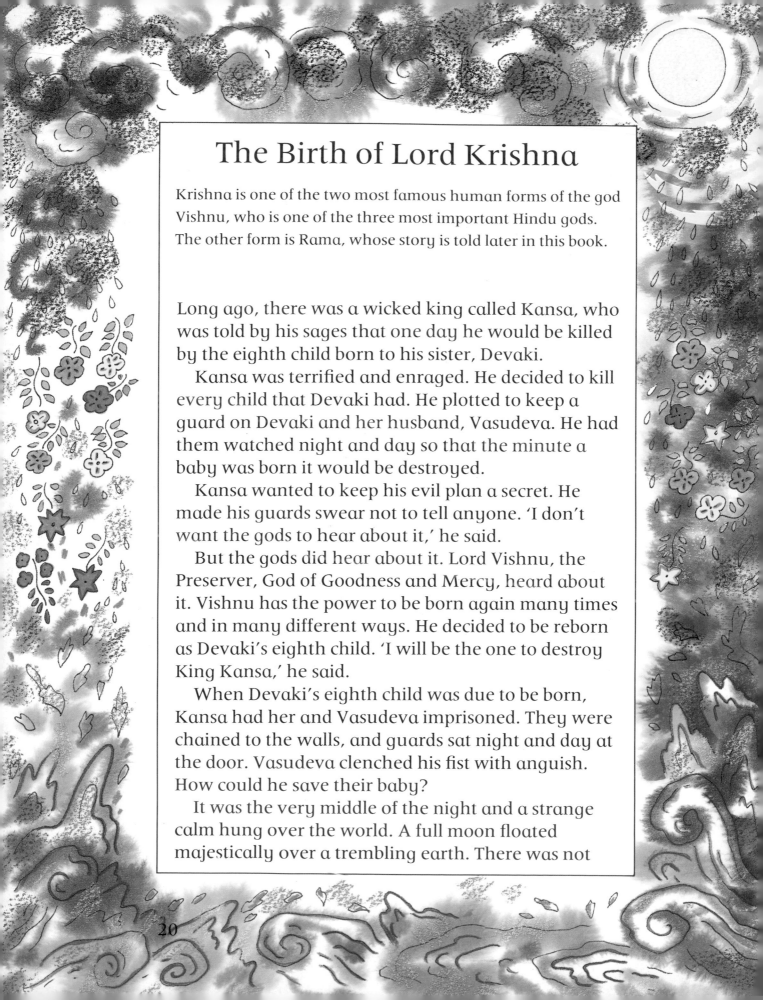

The Birth of Lord Krishna

Krishna is one of the two most famous human forms of the god Vishnu, who is one of the three most important Hindu gods. The other form is Rama, whose story is told later in this book.

Long ago, there was a wicked king called Kansa, who was told by his sages that one day he would be killed by the eighth child born to his sister, Devaki.

Kansa was terrified and enraged. He decided to kill every child that Devaki had. He plotted to keep a guard on Devaki and her husband, Vasudeva. He had them watched night and day so that the minute a baby was born it would be destroyed.

Kansa wanted to keep his evil plan a secret. He made his guards swear not to tell anyone. 'I don't want the gods to hear about it,' he said.

But the gods did hear about it. Lord Vishnu, the Preserver, God of Goodness and Mercy, heard about it. Vishnu has the power to be born again many times and in many different ways. He decided to be reborn as Devaki's eighth child. 'I will be the one to destroy King Kansa,' he said.

When Devaki's eighth child was due to be born, Kansa had her and Vasudeva imprisoned. They were chained to the walls, and guards sat night and day at the door. Vasudeva clenched his fist with anguish. How could he save their baby?

It was the very middle of the night and a strange calm hung over the world. A full moon floated majestically over a trembling earth. There was not even a breath of a wind to stir the dusty ground.

Suddenly, the moment arrived. Devaki's eighth child was born. As the dark, moist body of a boy wriggled into the world, a shiver of excitement vibrated round the universe. Up in heaven the drums thudded wildly. Lord Indra sent a shower of flowers and raindrops tumbling down out of the sky. All the devas and apsaras, the nymphs and the rishis burst into song. 'Lord Vishnu is reborn as a man, and his name is Krishna!'

Vasudeva held his son fearfully. Everyone was asleep. The women who should have helped with the birth were snoring in a corner. Outside the prison door, the guards were slumped on the floor.

Suddenly the baby opened his eyes. It was like the windows of heaven opening. Devaki and Vasudeva found the chains had fallen from their bodies, and the locks on the door flew open.

'Quick! Escape! Save our baby!' cried Devaki.

Vasudeva gathered up baby Krishna. 'I'll take him somewhere safe,' he whispered.

With tears streaming down her face, Devaki kissed her child, then Vasudeva crept out into the night.

On the other side of the River Yamuna lived a cowherd and his wife called Nanda and Yasoda. They were good, honest people, and Vasudeva knew he could trust them. He hurried down to the river banks, and holding his baby close began to wade across.

Suddenly, a storm blew up. The waters swirled and began to rise higher and higher. Desperately, Vasudeva held the baby above his head. Just when he thought they must both drown, the baby Krishna

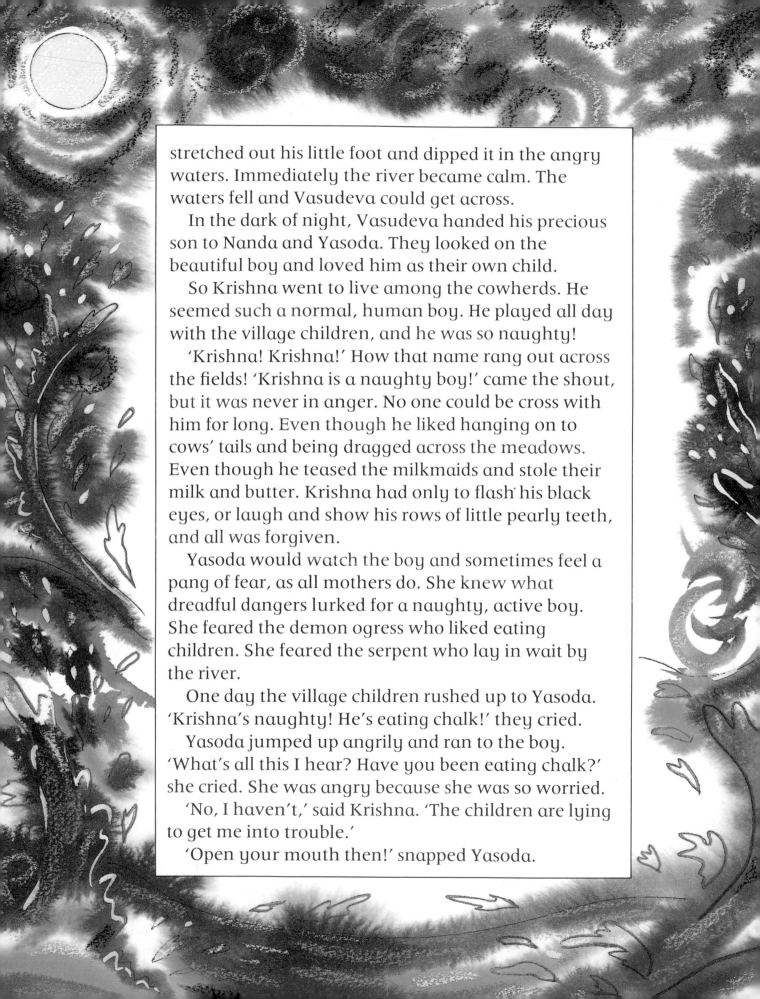

stretched out his little foot and dipped it in the angry waters. Immediately the river became calm. The waters fell and Vasudeva could get across.

In the dark of night, Vasudeva handed his precious son to Nanda and Yasoda. They looked on the beautiful boy and loved him as their own child.

So Krishna went to live among the cowherds. He seemed such a normal, human boy. He played all day with the village children, and he was so naughty!

'Krishna! Krishna!' How that name rang out across the fields! 'Krishna is a naughty boy!' came the shout, but it was never in anger. No one could be cross with him for long. Even though he liked hanging on to cows' tails and being dragged across the meadows. Even though he teased the milkmaids and stole their milk and butter. Krishna had only to flash his black eyes, or laugh and show his rows of little pearly teeth, and all was forgiven.

Yasoda would watch the boy and sometimes feel a pang of fear, as all mothers do. She knew what dreadful dangers lurked for a naughty, active boy. She feared the demon ogress who liked eating children. She feared the serpent who lay in wait by the river.

One day the village children rushed up to Yasoda. 'Krishna's naughty! He's eating chalk!' they cried.

Yasoda jumped up angrily and ran to the boy. 'What's all this I hear? Have you been eating chalk?' she cried. She was angry because she was so worried.

'No, I haven't,' said Krishna. 'The children are lying to get me into trouble.'

'Open your mouth then!' snapped Yasoda.

Krishna opened his mouth wide. Yasoda looked. Time and space stood still. Yasoda found herself gazing into the mouth of eternity. She saw all heaven and earth; the mountain ranges and rushing rivers. She saw the jungles and deserts and she even saw her own little village with the herdsmen in the fields. She saw the planets of the zodiac and the galaxies of the universe. She saw Earth, Water, Fire and Air. Yasoda gazed at creation itself in the mouth of Lord Vishnu.

In that moment, she understood. She knew that she didn't need to protect Krishna. He would protect her.

When Krishna shut his mouth, Yasoda immediately forgot what she had seen. But her heart overflowed with love for him. She took him on her lap, and she knew she would never be afraid again.

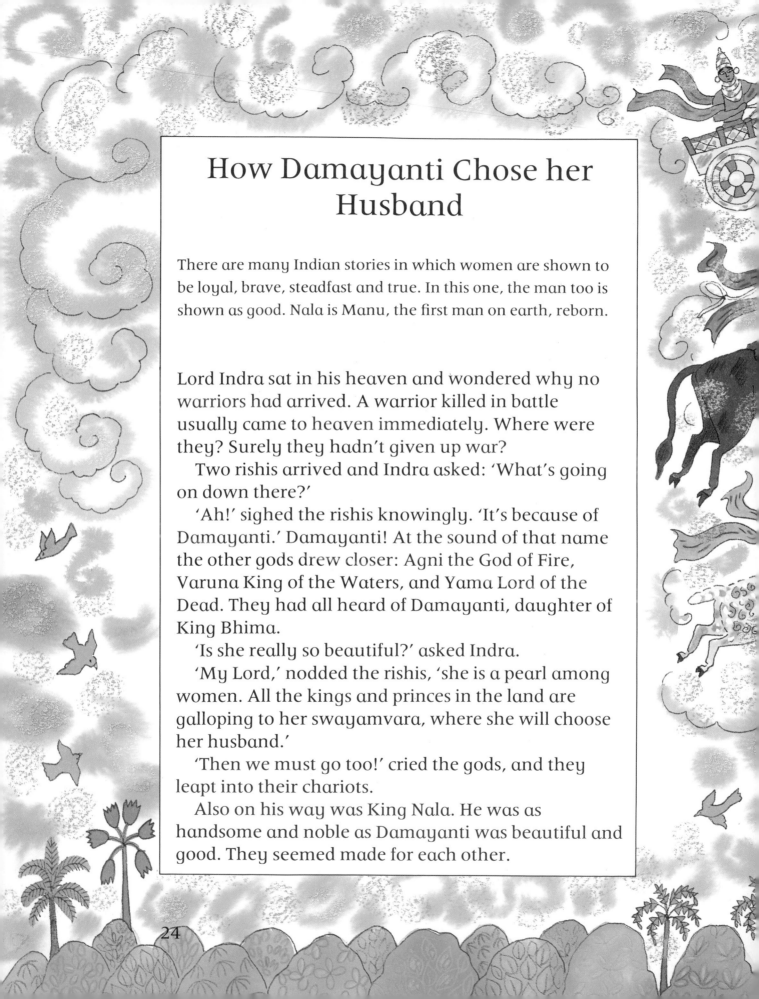

How Damayanti Chose her Husband

There are many Indian stories in which women are shown to be loyal, brave, steadfast and true. In this one, the man too is shown as good. Nala is Manu, the first man on earth, reborn.

Lord Indra sat in his heaven and wondered why no warriors had arrived. A warrior killed in battle usually came to heaven immediately. Where were they? Surely they hadn't given up war?

Two rishis arrived and Indra asked: 'What's going on down there?'

'Ah!' sighed the rishis knowingly. 'It's because of Damayanti.' Damayanti! At the sound of that name the other gods drew closer: Agni the God of Fire, Varuna King of the Waters, and Yama Lord of the Dead. They had all heard of Damayanti, daughter of King Bhima.

'Is she really so beautiful?' asked Indra.

'My Lord,' nodded the rishis, 'she is a pearl among women. All the kings and princes in the land are galloping to her swayamvara, where she will choose her husband.'

'Then we must go too!' cried the gods, and they leapt into their chariots.

Also on his way was King Nala. He was as handsome and noble as Damayanti was beautiful and good. They seemed made for each other.

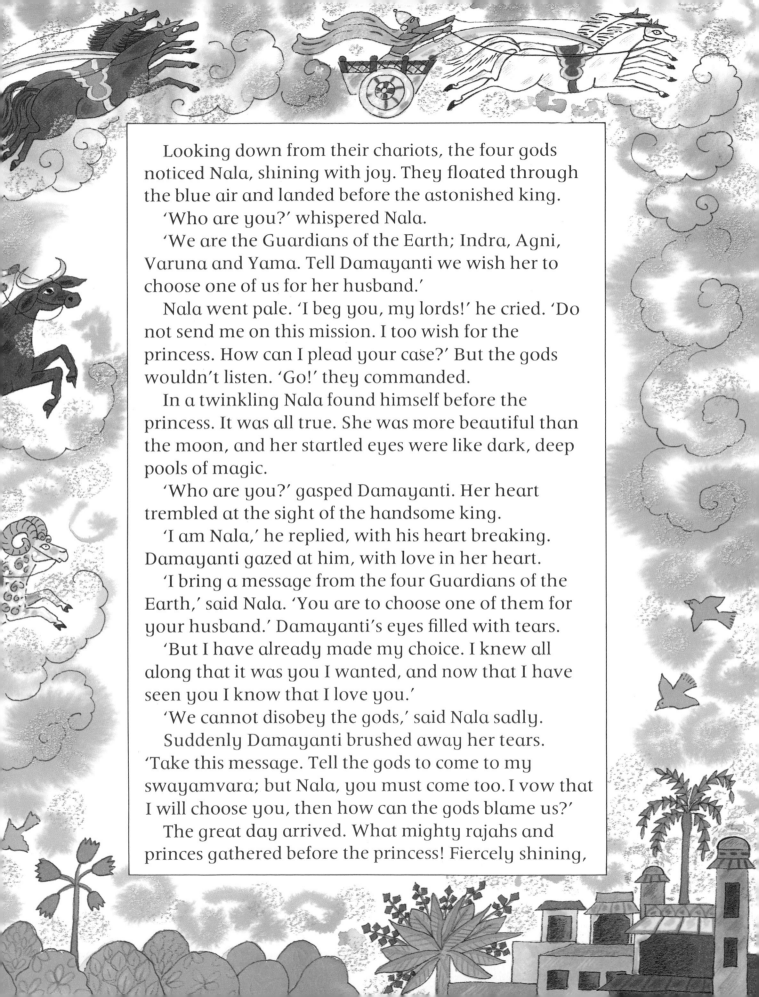

Looking down from their chariots, the four gods noticed Nala, shining with joy. They floated through the blue air and landed before the astonished king.

'Who are you?' whispered Nala.

'We are the Guardians of the Earth; Indra, Agni, Varuna and Yama. Tell Damayanti we wish her to choose one of us for her husband.'

Nala went pale. 'I beg you, my lords!' he cried. 'Do not send me on this mission. I too wish for the princess. How can I plead your case?' But the gods wouldn't listen. 'Go!' they commanded.

In a twinkling Nala found himself before the princess. It was all true. She was more beautiful than the moon, and her startled eyes were like dark, deep pools of magic.

'Who are you?' gasped Damayanti. Her heart trembled at the sight of the handsome king.

'I am Nala,' he replied, with his heart breaking. Damayanti gazed at him, with love in her heart.

'I bring a message from the four Guardians of the Earth,' said Nala. 'You are to choose one of them for your husband.' Damayanti's eyes filled with tears.

'But I have already made my choice. I knew all along that it was you I wanted, and now that I have seen you I know that I love you.'

'We cannot disobey the gods,' said Nala sadly.

Suddenly Damayanti brushed away her tears. 'Take this message. Tell the gods to come to my swayamvara; but Nala, you must come too. I vow that I will choose you, then how can the gods blame us?'

The great day arrived. What mighty rajahs and princes gathered before the princess! Fiercely shining, decked in jewels, they looked as magnificent as tigers. Some were proud, some were battle-scarred, some as smooth as serpents, and others glittering like stars. But Damayanti only looked for one face.

Suddenly she stopped in confusion. There was King Nala standing before her. But there he was again and again – five times! All were dressed alike, all looked at her with eyes brimming with love. The gods had tricked her. Damayanti clasped her hands in prayer.

'Oh my lords,' she prayed. 'Understand that I have chosen Nala for my husband. I made a holy vow. Help me to keep it. Show me Nala.'

Then the gods took pity on the princess and let her see the signs. The hot sun burned down on to the palace. In their flowing robes and jewels the rajahs began to perspire. The garlands of flowers wilted around their necks, and their garments grew dusty. But the four gods stayed dry, fresh and perfect.

Damayanti stared at the five Nalas. Four stared back at her unblinking, for gods never blink, but the fifth Nala moved his eyelids. Four had skin as dry as baked clay, but the fifth's face trickled with moisture. Across the floor the shadows of the waiting kings fell in black patterns. But four Nalas cast no shadows.

Damayanti's heart filled with hope. Slowly she looked at their feet. Four pairs of feet floated just a little off the ground, but the fifth Nala stood firmly on the marble floor. Damayanti flung her garland round his neck. 'King Nala! I choose you!'

So Nala and Damayanti were married, and the four gods rejoiced with them and gave them many heavenly gifts.

A Bargain with Death

Lord Yama is a judge who decides who shall live and who shall die. He also decides who goes to heaven and who goes to hell. As this story shows, it is possible to bargain with him.

Lord Yama, God of Death, played his flute beneath the cool, spreading shade of a tree. Silver notes floated through the shadowy groves of paradise. The brindled watchdog at the gate listened, his four eyes half closed. High in the branches, his companions the pigeon and the owl listened and waited. When Lord Yama stopped playing his messengers would collect the souls of those whose time had come. Lord Yama had the power over life and death, and he judged who should go to heaven and who to hell.

The music ceased. The dog sat up, poised and alert. The pigeon flapped, the owl hooted. It was time for some to face death. One of these was Pramadarva, a good and beautiful maiden.

Death was the last thing on Pramadarva's mind. She was to be married to the Brahman Ruru. The feast was planned, the musicians hired. But today she played with her friends. They chased among the trees.

Suddenly a fearful scream struck their hearts with terror. What was it? Then they saw Pramadarva standing as if frozen. A serpent slithered over her foot and disappeared into the thicket. With a low moan, she slid to the ground and died.

A cry rose up, 'Oh no! Not Pramadarva!'
Everyone gathered round her body. It didn't seem

possible. She looked more beautiful in death than in life. Heartbroken, Ruru cried out to the gods.

'If all the prayers and penances in my life mean anything, then bring my beloved back to life!'

A stillness fell and darkness covered the sun. Ruru raised his tear-stained face to see Lord Yama's messenger shimmering before him. 'Your prayers are useless,' said the messenger gently. 'Pramadarva died at the appointed time. Now I must take her soul.'

'Is there nothing I can do?' Ruru moaned.

'Pramadarva can live, if you will give her half your allotted life,' said the messenger.

Ruru gasped. 'I would give her half my life if I had only one day left,' he cried. 'I agree to the bargain!'

So the messenger went back to Lord Yama.

'My Lord,' he said, 'Ruru is willing to give up half his life to Pramadarva. Will you let her live?'

Lord Yama raised his flute and murmured, 'So be it.'

As Ruru rushed to her side, Pramadarva opened her eyes with wonderment.

'I dreamed I stood at the gates of heaven,' she said.

Soon the two were married, and never was there a sweeter or more loving couple. They lived their life together in great happiness, until Yama called them both to Paradise.

How Ganesh Got his Elephant's Head

Ganesh is one of India's most popular gods. His picture can be seen in homes, banks, shops and offices. He is the bringer of success and riches, and he is famous for his wisdom.

The goddess Parvati sat alone in her mountain palace waiting for her husband, Lord Shiva, to come home. She could see his distant figure on a high, snowy peak. He sat like a statue in a yoga position, praying. Would he never stop praying? He hardly seemed to know or care that she was there. She longed to be with him, and most of all, she longed for a child.

'Oh my Lord!' she wailed. 'God of Gods! Blue-throated and three-eyed! I do so wish for a child!' But Lord Shiva only heaved a sigh of irritation and left.

Parvati wept with frustration. Fretfully, she went out on to the mountain-side and played with the soft earth. She squeezed the clay in her hands as she tried to forget her sadness. A body took shape in her hands. She modelled the rounded limbs, and delicately picked out the features of its face. At last a beautiful, baby boy lay in her lap. How lovingly she gazed at its blank face and stroked its stiff body! She held it in her arms and murmured:

'Live! Live! Be my baby!'

As she spoke a smile, as radiant as a softly opening lotus, spread across his face. He opened round, black, glistening eyes and cried, 'Mama! Mama!'

Parvati sang for joy. She called her son Ganesh. He grew with such power that soon he was guardian at the gate, and his mother's most fierce protector. And so, for some time, they lived happily together.

Then one day, Lord Shiva returned. He hadn't heard about Ganesh, and the child did not know his father. As Shiva entered the palace, Ganesh tried to stop him. Angrily, Lord Shiva turned his third eye on him, and Ganesh's head was struck off.

Parvati's sorrow was dreadful. Her screams of horror and grief echoed round the mountains.'My baby! My baby! You've killed my baby!'

'Don't grieve, Parvati!' soothed Lord Shiva. 'I'll put things right. Ganesh shall have the head of the first living thing that is found facing north.'

Messengers were sent throughout the universe. Suddenly one of them saw a mighty elephant, and his head was turned to the north. Although it was Indra's own elephant, the messenger struck off its head and took it to Shiva, who joyfully placed it on Ganesh's shoulders. Parvati thought her child looked beautiful. Now he would have wisdom, knowledge and kindness.

As his chubby body breathed once more, bees hummed round him as if he were a flower. With his four arms, and round belly, and his shining, moon-bright head, he was called 'Gajanana' – elephant face – and was everyone's friend.

The Story of Rama and Sita

Stories of Rama and Sita were told in India for centuries before anyone wrote them down. Rama is the god Vishnu in human form. He is a perfect hero – brave, honest and kind.

The golden deer gazed innocently among the trees. It was a calm day, and a sense of peace hung over the forest. As the animal moved delicately through the grass, the silver spots on its body shone like little moons, and the sapphire tips of its horns sparkled in the sunlight.

Nearby, Princess Sita wandered into the grove picking wild flowers and singing softly. Her husband, Prince Rama, and his brother, Lakshmana, were sitting outside their hut of branches and twigs.

Ever since Rama had been forced into exile from his kingdom, the three of them had learned to survive the dangers of the forest.

A faint rustle made Sita look up. She found herself

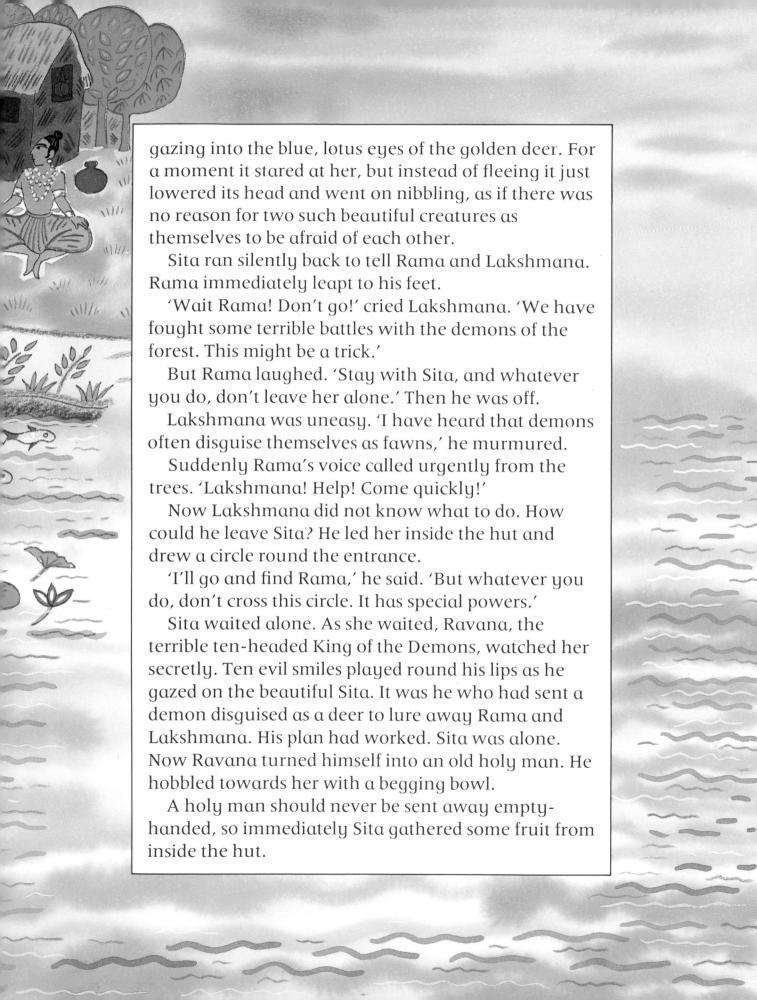

gazing into the blue, lotus eyes of the golden deer. For a moment it stared at her, but instead of fleeing it just lowered its head and went on nibbling, as if there was no reason for two such beautiful creatures as themselves to be afraid of each other.

Sita ran silently back to tell Rama and Lakshmana. Rama immediately leapt to his feet.

'Wait Rama! Don't go!' cried Lakshmana. 'We have fought some terrible battles with the demons of the forest. This might be a trick.'

But Rama laughed. 'Stay with Sita, and whatever you do, don't leave her alone.' Then he was off.

Lakshmana was uneasy. 'I have heard that demons often disguise themselves as fawns,' he murmured.

Suddenly Rama's voice called urgently from the trees. 'Lakshmana! Help! Come quickly!'

Now Lakshmana did not know what to do. How could he leave Sita? He led her inside the hut and drew a circle round the entrance.

'I'll go and find Rama,' he said. 'But whatever you do, don't cross this circle. It has special powers.'

Sita waited alone. As she waited, Ravana, the terrible ten-headed King of the Demons, watched her secretly. Ten evil smiles played round his lips as he gazed on the beautiful Sita. It was he who had sent a demon disguised as a deer to lure away Rama and Lakshmana. His plan had worked. Sita was alone. Now Ravana turned himself into an old holy man. He hobbled towards her with a begging bowl.

A holy man should never be sent away empty-handed, so immediately Sita gathered some fruit from inside the hut.

'Here take this!' she cried, stretching out her hands.

'Alas! A holy man cannot receive gifts from inside a home. You must come over here,' sighed the old man.

Sita hesitated. Surely a holy man couldn't do her harm? Convinced there was nothing to fear, she crossed the circle. With a roar the evil king sprang upon her like a tiger on its prey.

'Now you are mine!' he bellowed.

Sita screamed and struggled as Ravana dragged her to his chariot. But it was no use. The chariot rose into the air, and flew away over the forest.

Rama realized he had been tricked. He was grief-stricken. He and Lakshmana ran through the forest yelling for Sita. They stumbled upon Jatayu, King of the Vultures. His body was broken, his beak smashed.

'I tried to stop him,' he choked, 'Ravana has taken your Sita.'

Rama wept. 'Which way did they go?'

'Southwards,' whispered the faithful Jatayu, with his dying breath.

And so began the long search for Sita. Battling with hardship and danger, through jungle and plain they travelled, until one day, just as the rainy season was starting, they arrived at the mountain kingdom of Sugriva, the Ape.

'We saw Ravana's chariot flying to the island of Lanka,' said the ape king. 'If Sita is a prisoner there, you will need my armies of apes and bears to rescue her. Ravana's forces are mighty and terrible.'

Then Hanuman, Sugriva's general and counsellor stepped forward. 'Let me go to Lanka. I'll find out where Sita is being kept.'

Rama could have no better friend than Hanuman. This ape son of Vayu, the Wind God, was brave and swift. He could change into any size or shape. He was clever and cunning, but above all he was faithful.

Magically he transported himself by night to the island of Lanka, and soon stood in the heart of the Demon King's glittering palace. He changed himself into a black cat and padded from chamber to chamber in search of Sita. Up stairways of silver and gold, across sparkling floors of crystal he went, but nowhere could he find Sita. Then he leaped out on to the highest wall in the city and looked around. Suddenly, he noticed a faint light in a grove in the gardens. Turning back into a monkey he sprang into the branches and swung through the trees. He had found her at last.

Sita sat beneath a tree. She looked worn with weeping. She was surrounded with evil-headed demons who dozed and grunted in the moonless night. Silently, Hanuman dropped to the ground before her.

'Sita!' he whispered, 'I come from Rama, he is going to rescue you.'

Sita stifled a cry of joy. When Hanuman saw her tear-stained face he was enraged with the demons. He gave a roar of fury. He began to grow and grow until he towered like a tree above them. He rushed at the demons clawing and scratching, smashing and uprooting. But finally he was captured. The demons dragged him before Ravana, shrieking 'Kill! Kill! Kill!' But Ravana said; 'No! Send him back disgraced. That will show our enemies how helpless they are.'

So they got a fiery brand and set fire to Hanuman's long, fine tail.

At once Hanuman changed size, and made himself small enough to slip out of his bonds. With triumphant cries he sprang from roof to roof with his burning tail, setting the city alight from end to end. Then he sucked his tail to put the fire out and sped back to Sugriva.

Sugriva summoned his forces.

Great bears came lumbering. Apes of green, blue, yellow and red massed behind the gleaming king. With nails like swords and arrow-like teeth, they looked a dreadful army.

'Victory to Rama!' they cheered and rushed down to the ocean. The island of Lanka gleamed like a jewel across the waves. How would they get there? They set to work to build a bridge. Hurling rocks and boulders into the sea, it took them five days. Then, Sugriva's armies surged across like a tidal wave.

The battle raged. Rama knew that he alone must fight the final battle with Ravana. He took up his mighty bow and sheath of arrows. Through the lashing armies and smoke of battle the Demon King's

twenty eyes blazed. He charged towards Rama, his ten heads glowering with hatred. Rama shot arrow after arrow at each head, but no sooner was one head struck off than another grew in its place. Then Rama took up the flaming arrow tip given to him by Lord Brahma himself. He aimed at the Demon King and fired. Ravana's ten heads swung in howls of fearful agony, and he died.

At last the battle was won. The apes tenderly brought Sita out of the city and led her to Rama. With tears of joy she knelt at his feet.

The air was filled with the rushing of angels' wings and tumbling flowers. 'Rama, Rama, Sita, Rama!' cried everyone. 'The battle is won, the exile over.'

Rama, Sita and Lakshmana said goodbye to their loving and faithful friends, and returned home triumphantly. At last Rama could be crowned king and Sita his queen, and peace and prosperity returned once more to their kingdom.

How the River Ganga Came to Earth

This story tells how, once again, Lord Shiva leaps forward to save the world from disaster. It also tells of the goddess Ganga – in whose waters people bathe, pray, heal themselves and cast their ashes after death.

The goddess Ganga, a mighty river, lived in the heavenly regions of the Himalayas. She was the most sacred of rivers. Those who bathed in her waters were cleansed of their sins and gained everlasting life. Yet if it hadn't been for King Sagara the Ganga might never have come to earth.

King Sagara had two wives but no children. He prayed so devotedly that at last he was rewarded. One wife had one son, and the other had thousands.

To show his gratitude to the gods, the king wanted to make a most important sacrifice – a horse. He took the finest he could find, but it belonged to Lord Indra. Before it was slaughtered, Indra stole it away.

Sagara searched the world for this horse. His sons searched too, and finally began to dig towards the centre of the earth to see if it was there. The Earth goddess, wife of Lord Vishnu, cried in pain as the sons dug deeper. So Vishnu sent a terrible fire which burned Sagara's sons to death.

The king was grief-stricken. He hadn't meant to offend anyone. He begged the gods to return his sons.

'Your sons will come back to life and go to heaven,' he was told, 'when the River Ganga flows to earth.'

So once more Sagara began to pray. At last, Lord Brahma allowed Ganga to flow to earth.

The river gathered into a mighty torrent, her massive weight ready to hurl down on the earth below. Suddenly, Lord Shiva realized that the whole world would be engulfed if the river wasn't broken up first. As the great mass began to fall, he stood underneath. Ganga fell on to the god's head and was trapped in his tangled hair. She was unable to escape, until Shiva divided her up into seven streams.

With a roar like thunder the seven rivers of Ganga came streaming down through the sky. Fish and turtles came tumbling down, and spray which scattered like white birds. Gods, angels and heavenly warriors watched in amazement. Their jewels reflected in the drops of water and sparkled like suns.

Ganga fell to earth, and the seven rivers broke up into brooks and streams, waterfalls and pools. They rushed merrily through rocks and gulleys, and dashed down on to the hot, thirsty, Indian plain.

The water trickled through the earth until it reached the ashes of Sagara's sons. As water and ashes mingled, they came to life, and their souls rose rejoicing to heaven. Now the Ganga flows on earth, and everyone who bathes in her waters will have everlasting life.

The Hatred that Led to War

Every year, this story of rivalry between the Pandavas and the Kauravas is acted and danced in the towns and villages of India. Like many other Hindu stories, it dates back many hundreds of years.

In the dead of night the young princess Pritha secretly placed her new-born son in a basket. Full of shame and sorrow, she took the basket to the river and let it float away on the current. She prayed to the gods to care for her child.

   The boy was found by a charioteer and his wife who brought him up as their own. They named him Karna. They didn't know he was a prince, and that his father was the Sun God, Surya.

   Later, Princess Pritha married the great King Pandu. She bore him five sons who became known as the Pandavas. Pandu had become king because his elder brother, Dhritarashtra, was blind.

   Dhritarashtra had a hundred sons, and they became known as the Kauravas.

Even when they were children growing up together, the Pandavas and the Kauravas were great rivals. The boys grew to manhood, learning all the skills of princes. They became fine archers, swordsmen and hunters. But the Pandavas outshone the rest, and the Kauravas grew jealous.

One day there was a magnificent tournament. Everyone in the land was invited to take part. Once again, the Pandava brothers showed their unmatched skill and bravery.

Just when it seemed that the tournament was over, a stranger appeared in golden armour. He marched up to Arjuna, the bravest and finest of the Pandava brothers. He challenged him, crying:

'I can perform any skill that you can – and better! Let me prove it!'

It was true. The mysterious warrior was every bit as good as Arjuna, and the Kauravas were delighted.

'Let us now fight in equal combat!' exclaimed the strange newcomer.

Queen Pritha fainted with anguish and despair, for she had recognized her first born son, Karna. She was torn with secret grief to see her two sons facing each other in mortal combat.

But before they could fight, darkness fell. It was time to make offerings and pray to the gods. Everyone left the tournament, some saying that Arjuna was the victor, others that it was Karna.

When finally they fought, the battle was longer and far more bloody than any tournament. What greater evil could stalk the earth than the hatred between brothers and cousins? The god, Krishna, tried to bring peace. He went to Karna and said:

'I know you were wronged by your mother, but come with me now to the Pandavas. Tell them everything, and they will regard you as their elder brother.' But Karna was allied with the Kauravas, and would not go.

Krishna sent a message to Karna and the Kauravas.

'Let it be known,' he said, 'that I, Krishna shall be Arjuna's charioteer when he rides into battle.'

The vast battleground fluttered from end to end with flags. The sun glinted on shields and spears, as the chariots of princes and warriors lined up against each other. Arjuna said to Krishna:

'Drive me down to a place between the two armies.'

Krishna gathered the reins of the five white horses as if he gathered in his five senses, and galloped down to the plain.

Arjuna gazed all around him. He recognized everyone. They were his own flesh and blood; fathers and grandfathers; sons and grandsons; brothers and uncles. They were his kinsmen. He dropped his warrior's bow, and fell back, grief stricken. 'Ah Krishna!' he wept.

'I have no stomach for this war. I seek no victory. How can I rejoice in the death of my kinsmen? Oh day of darkness! How have we come to this?'

But Krishna said, 'What you see is not the truth. You are not fighting mortals, you are fighting evil, and this is a battle which must be won. Death is just throwing off an old garment to put on a new one. Trust in me, Arjuna, for I am the Light!'

So began the Battle of Eighteen Days. At each pale

dawn the warriors faced each other; at each red sunset the battlefield was running with blood.

At last the Kauravas were defeated. Karna was killed and the enemy scattered. Although the Pandavas were victorious, they could not celebrate. They cast off their royal garments and set off on a long pilgrimage to the sacred mountain of Meru.

One by one they died on the way, but only to find themselves welcomed in heaven by Lord Indra and Lord Krishna. There too was Karna and their cousins the Kauravas. Now they could forget their quarrels.

They embraced each other, and entered together through the shining doors of the Celestial City.

Background Notes

How the World Began

In Hinduism, there is no one creation and no one destruction. The life and death cycle of humanity is a microcosm of the life and death cycle of the universe. It is a never-ending process, like the turning of a wheel. Our knowledge and memory can only go back to the latest creation.

This story comes from the *Rig Veda* (one of the four earliest Hindu scriptures), which was written at least 4000 years ago. Here the poets tried to imagine what it was like when there was nothing. They wrote of Lord Brahma, the World Soul, the All in All.

There are many Hindu creation stories. This is one of the oldest and simplest, where Lord Brahma is the First Cause of Everything. When he sleeps, there is nothing. When he wakes, he creates the universe all over again. So he is called The Creator. He rides on a swan.

How Lord Shiva Became Blue-throated

The account of how Lord Shiva became blue-throated goes back to the earliest creation stories and the churning of the Sea of Milk. The story is symbolic in two ways. First, it emphasizes Lord Shiva as the counterpart of Brahma. Brahma is the Creator, and Shiva is the destroyer of evil and the defender of goodness. Brahma and Shiva form a trinity with Lord Vishnu, the Preserver.

Secondly, the churning of the Sea of Milk is a link with the Hindu devotion to the cow. Lord Brahma created the cow by drinking nectar after the churning of the Sea. Milk from the cow is churned to produce butter, curds and cheese.

Indra, the Dragon-slayer

The *Rig Veda* sings of the god Indra, the great warrior god, the God of Nature, the bringer of rain and fighter of the drought demons. Lord Indra is also Lord of Heaven. He lives on Mount Meru, somewhere in the Himalayas, between Heaven and Earth. Although he is noisy and boisterous, he is very popular, for in a land of heat and drought, the bringer of rain is the bringer of life itself.

Manu's Ark

Manu was the first man to live on earth. He made the first laws and was the first to offer sacrifices to the gods. He was 'mindborn' of Brahma – which means that Brahma only had to think of him and Manu was born from his thoughts. A 'rishi' is someone who is mindborn. He is human, but he has special powers. Manu, for example, was able to stand on one leg and pray for ten thousand years.

How Lord Agni Tried to Hide

It is also in the *Rig Veda* that we first hear of Lord Agni, who is one of the most important of the gods. As the God of Fire, he is the spark of life – the creator of the sun as well as the humble fire in the hearth at home. He is the messenger between heaven and earth, for in his sacrificial flame, the sins of the world are purified. He rides on a ram.

The Birth of Lord Krishna

In recent times, Vishnu has become especially important in the Hindu trinity. Two of the most famous incarnations are Krishna and Rama. The story of the birth of Krishna is in some ways like the story of the birth of Jesus. In both stories, the birth was foretold, and in both a wicked king threatened the child's life. Both Krishna and Jesus were brought up in humble homes.

How Damayanti Chose her Husband

This story, like many of the famous myths and legends of India, is contained within the collection of heroic tales known as the *Mahabharata*. This came into being at least 3000 years ago.

A swayamvara is a ceremony where a young woman chooses a husband from all her suitors. They gather together for the occasion, as this story describes.

A Bargain with Death

This ancient Aryan folk tale is preserved within the *Mahabharata*. As Lord of the Dead, Yama is the first guide from the living world to the Land of the Dead. His skin is green and he wears a dark red garment. On his head is a crown with a flower in his hair. He carries a noose with which to trap the souls of the dead. He rides on a buffalo.

How Ganesh Got his Elephant's Head

This story touchingly describes the loneliness of a wife who is unfortunate enough to have a husband whose mind is always on higher things. It also shows how deadly Shiva can be when he is defied – as well as how merciful he can be when he wants to put things right. Ganesh is popular because he brings success, and is famous for his wisdom and friendliness. Few people set out on a task without first making a prayer to Ganesh.

The Story of Rama and Sita

For centuries, stories of Rama and Sita have been told by actors, dancers, singers and story-tellers – long before anyone wrote them down. They appear in the great book which became known as the *Ramayana*. The author of this book was the poet, Valmiki, who was told it by a famous rishi called Narada.

Rama is full of courage, honesty and tenderness – but he has some failings within the human guise. He is what every mother looks for in a son, and every wife hopes for in a husband. When Gandhi was shot, he died with the name Rama on his lips. At the core of the story is the love of Rama and Sita for each other. The story describes Rama's anguish when Sita is captured by demons and he begins a long, long search for his beloved.

How the River Ganga Came to Earth

The River Ganga unites the Hindu trinity of Brahma, Vishnu and Shiva. This greatest and holiest of Indian rivers is the fifth head of Brahma; she flows out of the toe of Vishnu and her fall to earth is broken by Lord Shiva, who catches her in his hair.

The Hatred that Led to War

The core of the stories in the *Mahabharata* deals with the rivalry between two families, the Kauravas and their cousins the Pandavas. This brief extract outlines just one thread and gives an introduction to this magnificent saga. The high point of this story, and of the *Mahabharata* itself, is the famous conversation between Arjuna and Krishna. This is often published separately and is known as the *Bhagavadgita*. It expresses with great power and beauty the philosophy and teaching of Vishnu, of whom Krishna is an incarnation.

A note about names

The spellings of Hindu names used in this book represent those conventionally used in publications in English. In fact, from a phonetic point of view, they are really rather misleading. English spellings of names such as Rama, Shiva and Nala, for example, suggest two syllable pronunciation, with an 'a' sound at the end. But Indians more usually pronounce them as one-syllable names: Ram, Shiv and Nal.